KINDERGARTEN MATH WORKBOOK

FORD PRESS

TABLE OF CONTENT

Name: ________________________________ **Score:** ______________

Count, color and write the numeral and number of objects in words

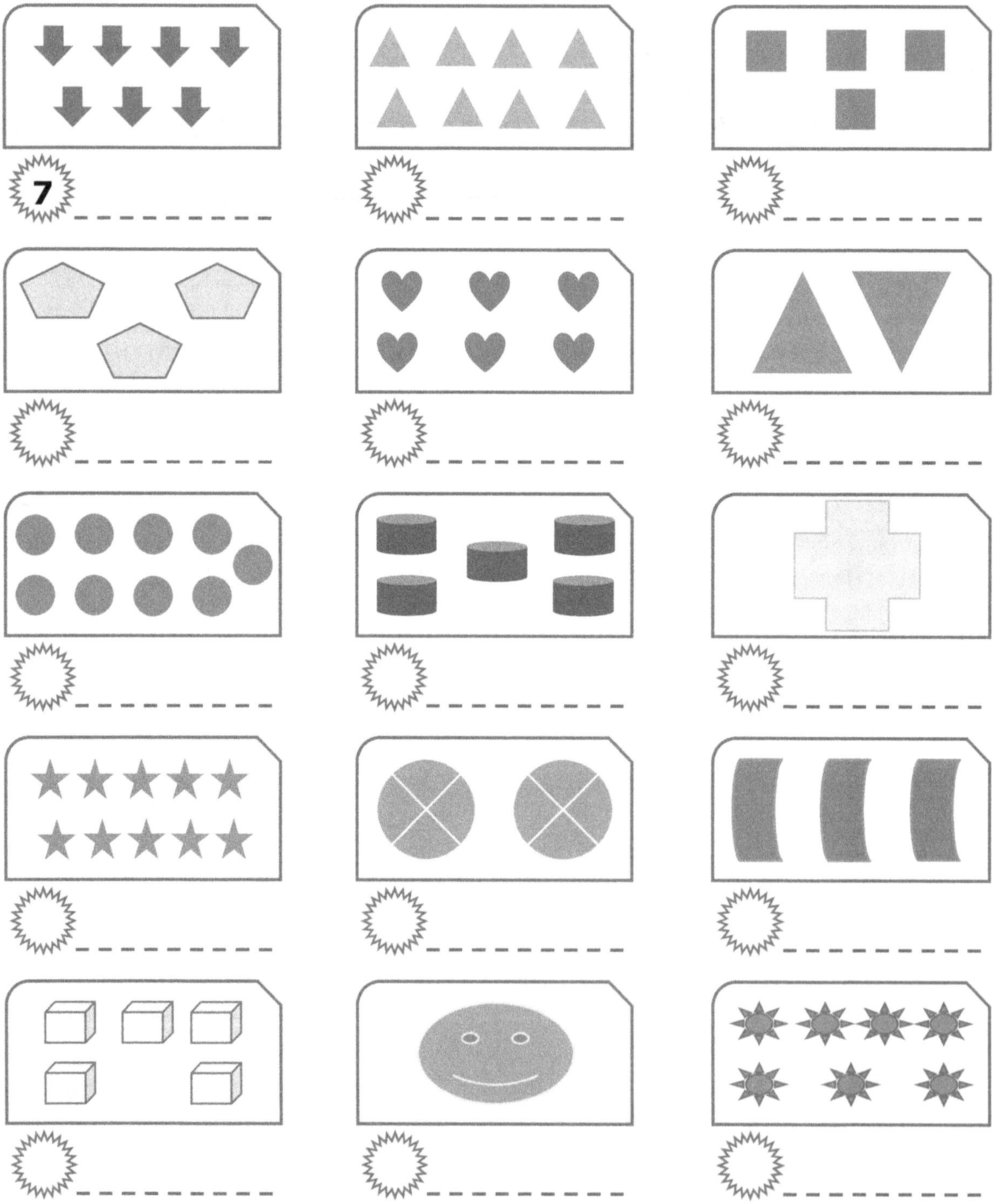

7

COUNT AND WRITE NUMBERS

Name: _________________________________ **Score:** ______________

Count, color and write the numeral and number of objects in words

Name: _________________________________ **Score:** _______________

Count the animals and answer the questions

1) How many fish can you see? _____

2) How man duck can you see? _____

3) How many more fish than duck can you count? _____

4) How many more fish than cat can you count? _____

5) How many cats can you count? _____

6) How many animals that can swim can you count? _____

COUNTING ANIMALS

Name: ________________________________ **Score:** _______________

Count the animals and answer the questions

1) How many frogs can you count? _____

2) How man owl can you count? _____

3) How many more owls than tiger can you count? _____

4) How many more owls than dolphins can you count? _____

5) How many parrots can you count? _____

6) How many animals that are not owl can you count? _____

Name: _________________________________ **Score:** _______________

Count the number of pips (spots) for each sets of domino stones

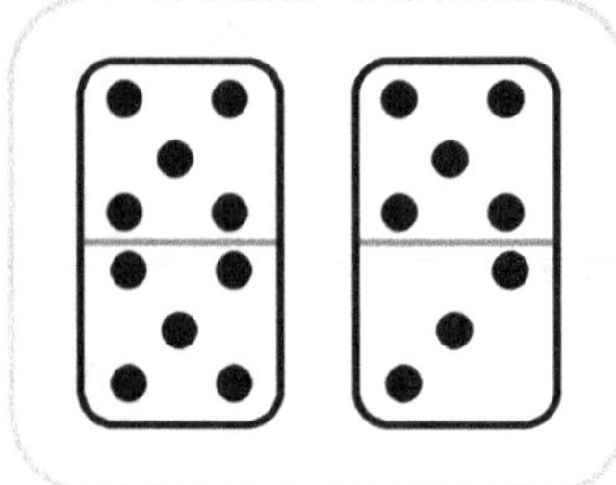

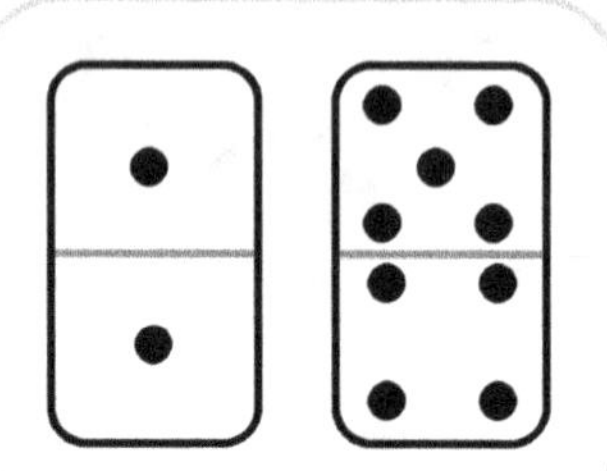

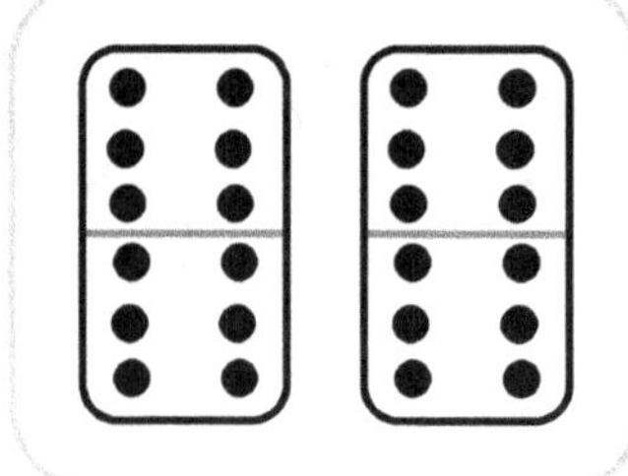

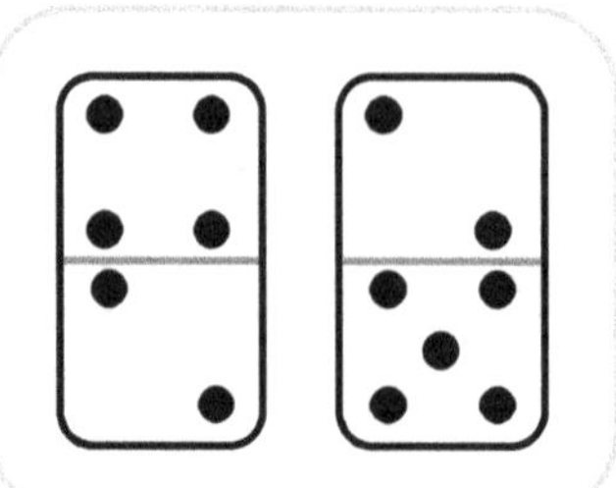

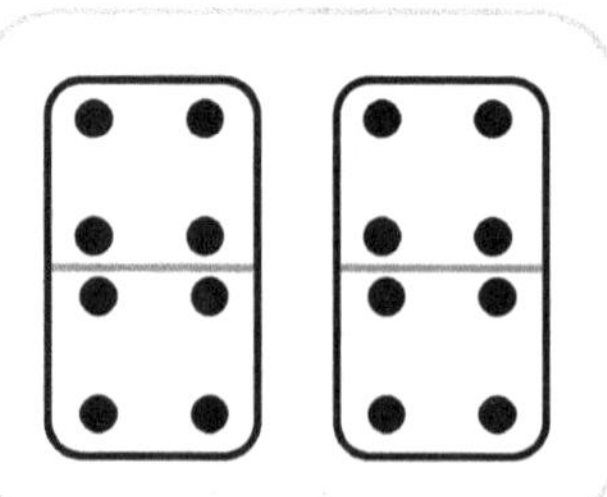

Name: _________________________________ **Score:** ________________

Count the number of pips (spots) for each sets of domino stones

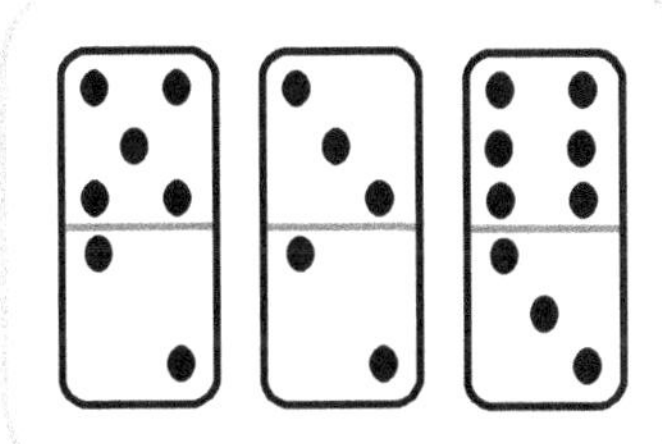  

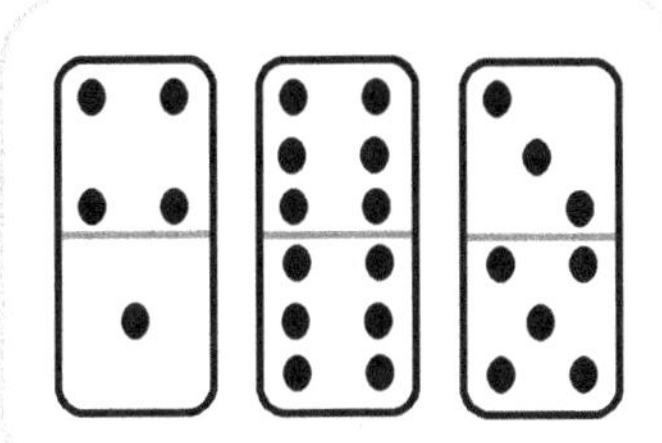 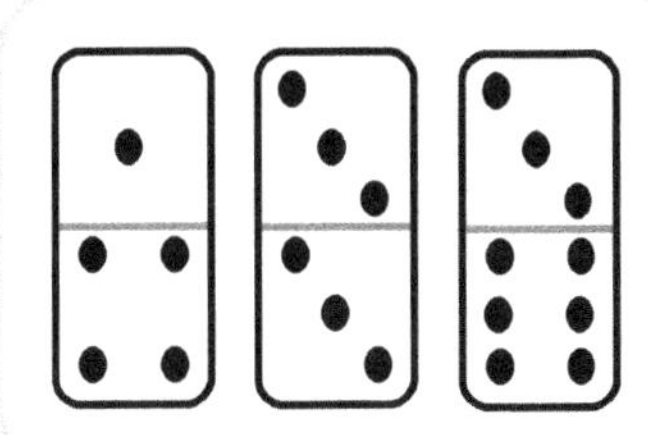 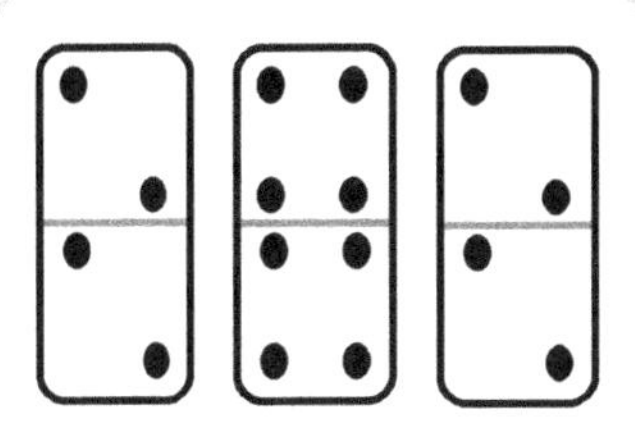

 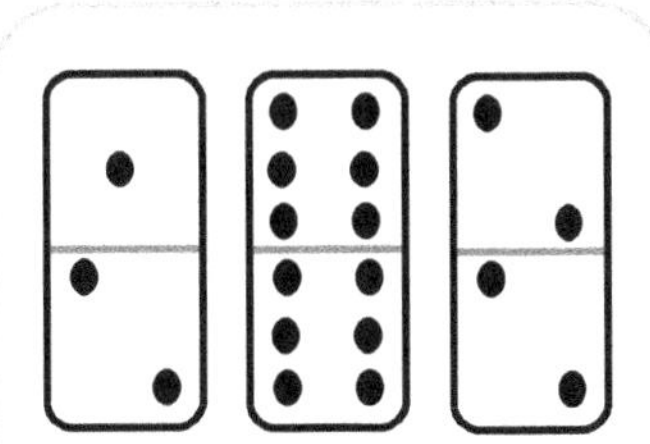 

Name: ______________________________ **Score:** ______________

Complete the number that comes before and after the numbers

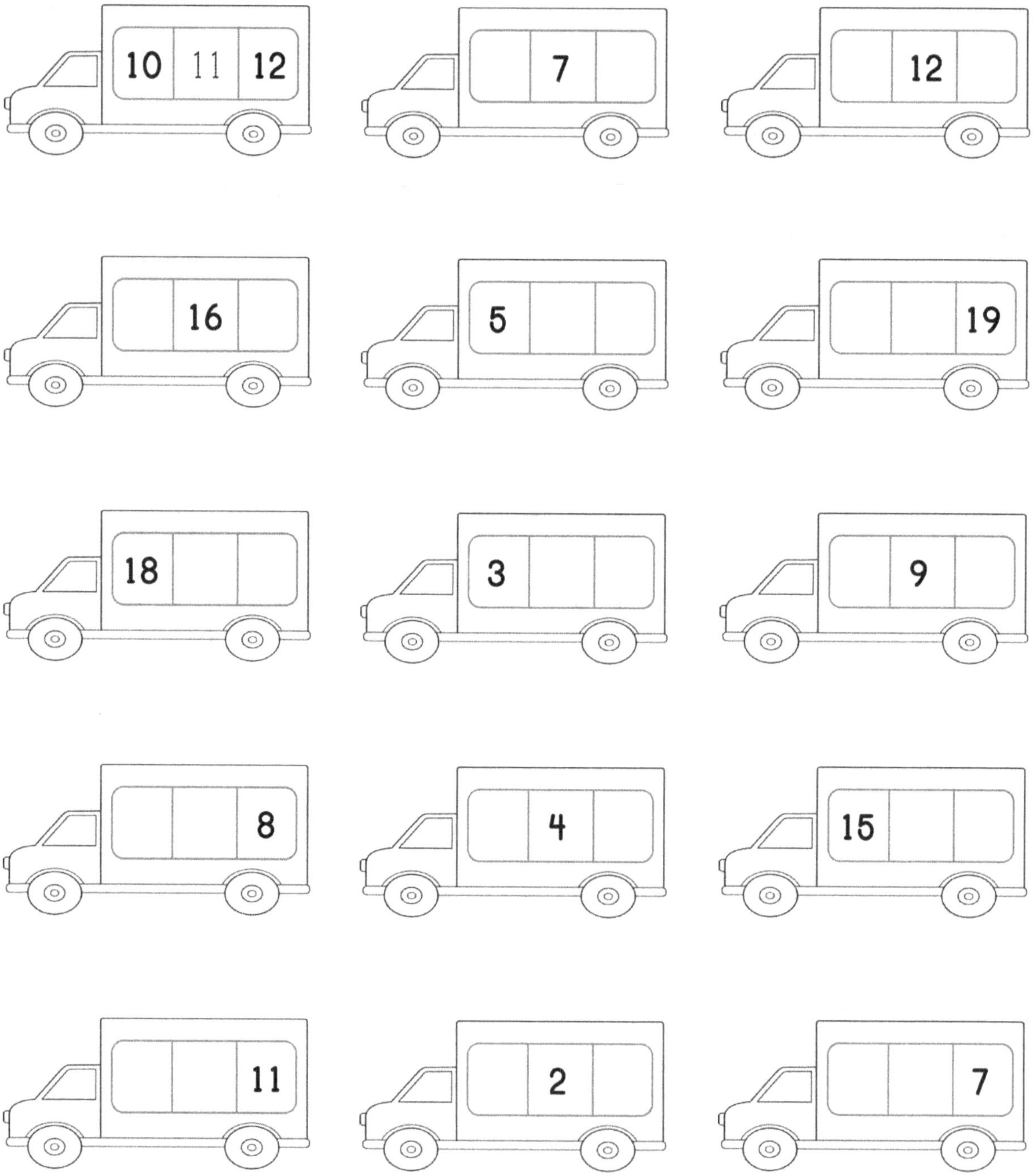

| 10 | 11 | 12 |

| | 7 | |

| | 12 | |

| 16 | | |

| 5 | | |

| | | 19 |

| 18 | | |

| 3 | | |

| | 9 | |

| | 8 | |

| 4 | | |

| 15 | | |

| | 11 | |

| 2 | | |

| | 7 | |

COUNTING NUMBERS UP TO 20

Name: _________________________________ **Score:** _______________

Count the numbers of cubes in each group

Name: _________________________________ **Score:** _______________

Count the numbers of domino dots

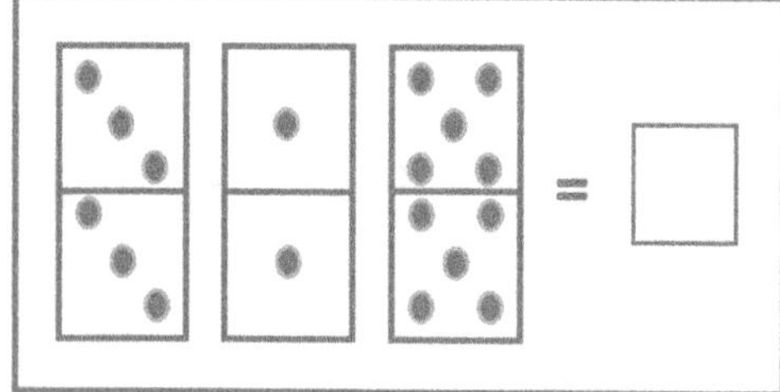 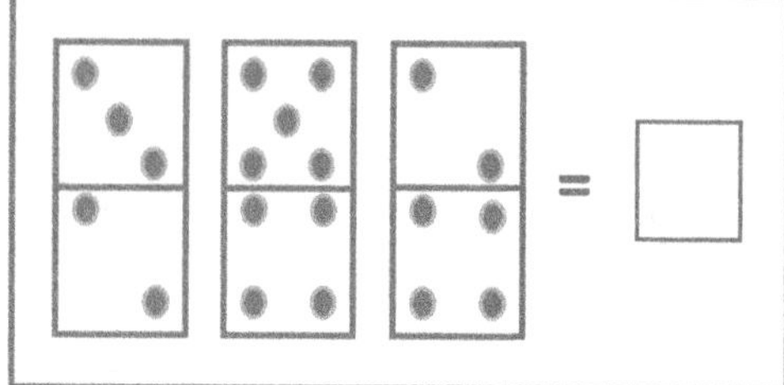

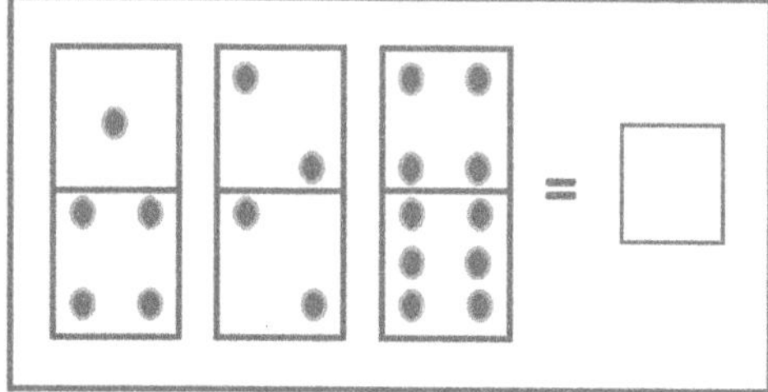 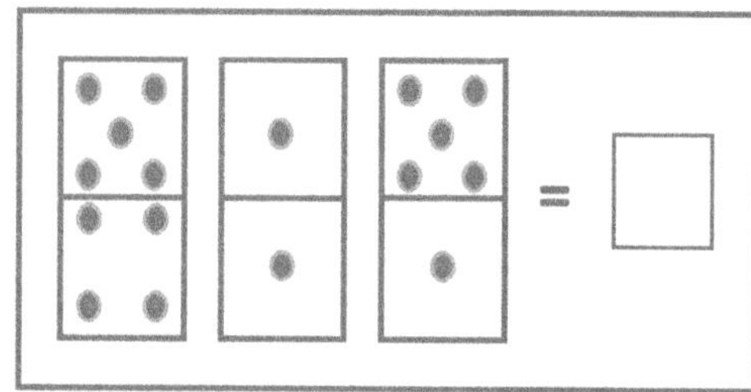

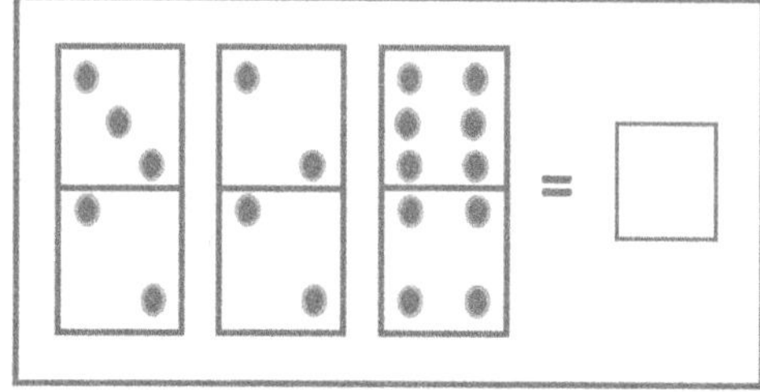 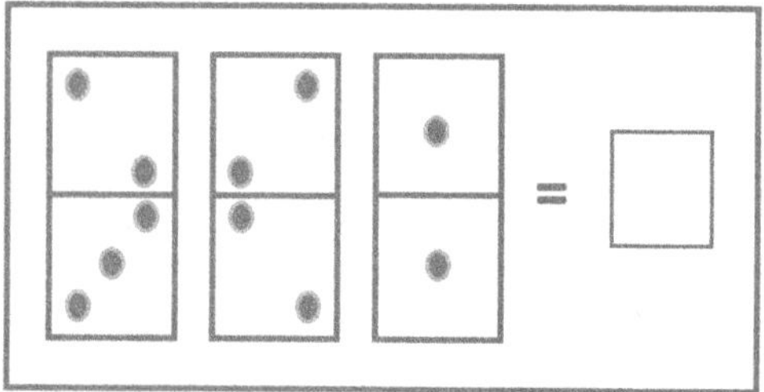

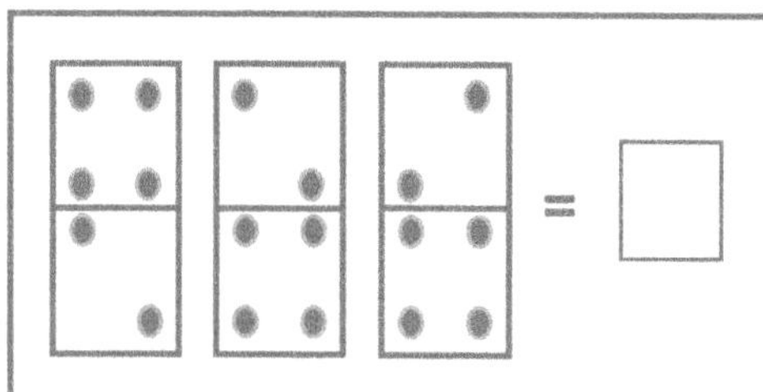 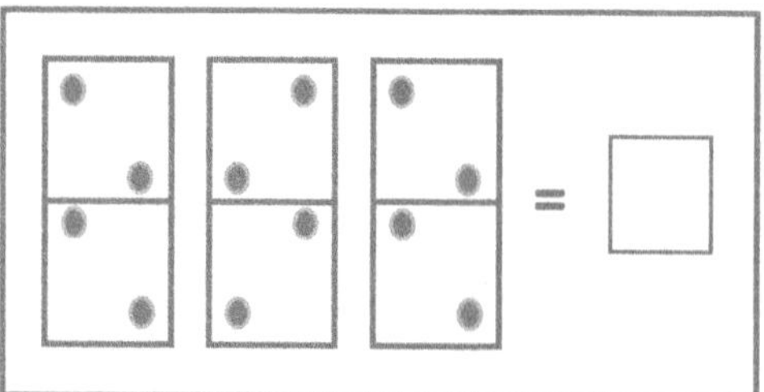

Name: _________________________________ **Score:** _______________

Count and write the numbers of each shape below

a) How many more squares are there more than triangles? _______
b) How many more circles are there more than rectangles? _______
c) How many more stars are there more than triangles? _______
d) How many more triangles are there more than circles? _______

Name: ___________________________________ **Score:** _______________

Color or shade the given number of objects

12

17

20

10

15

COUNTING FORWARD

Name: _________________________________ **Score:** _____________

Count forward in each row and complete the empty spaces

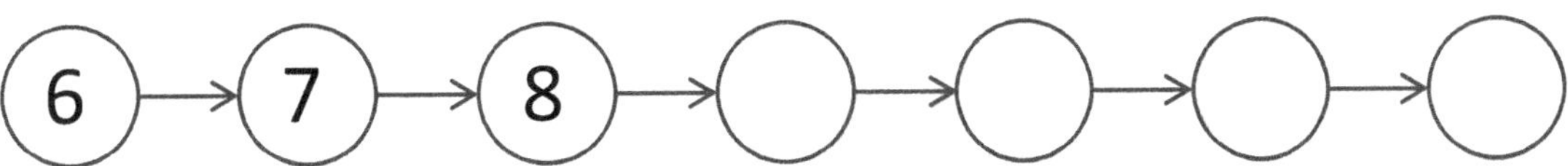

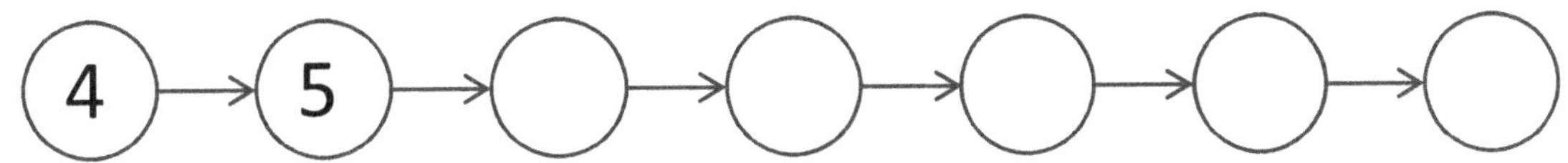

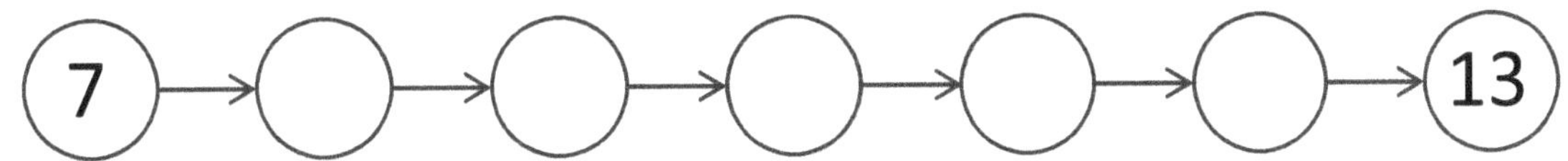

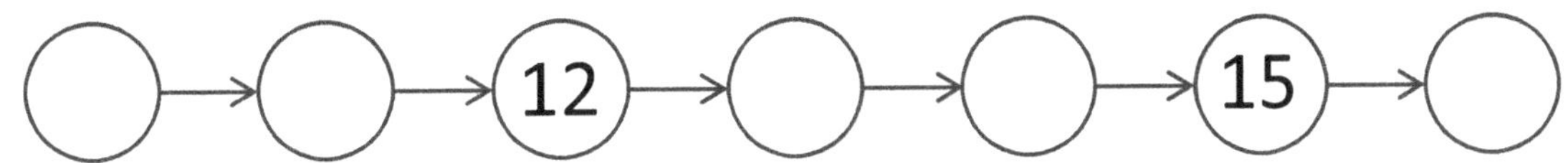

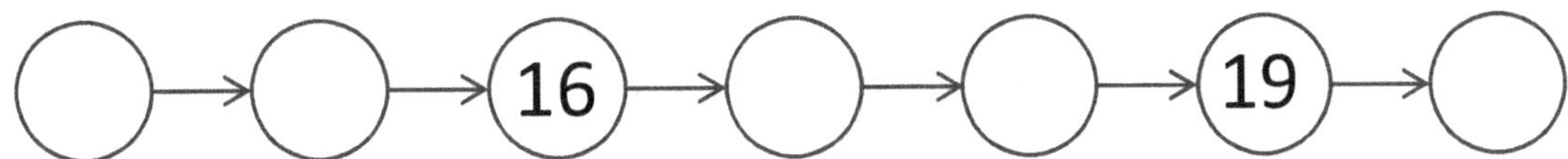

COUNTING BACKWARD

Name: _________________________________ **Score:** _______________

Count backward in each row and complete the empty spaces

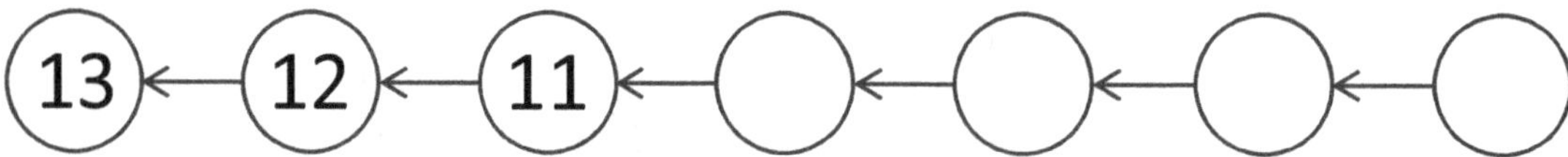

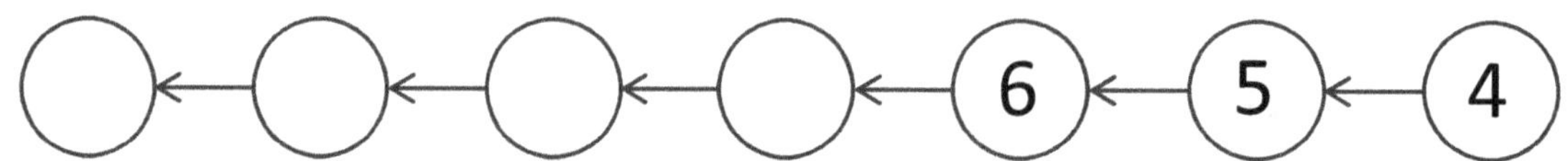

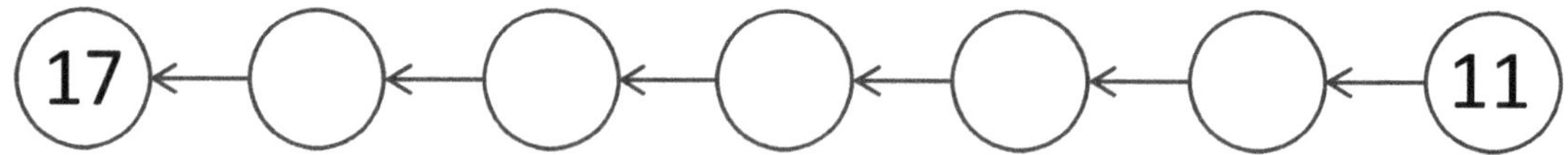

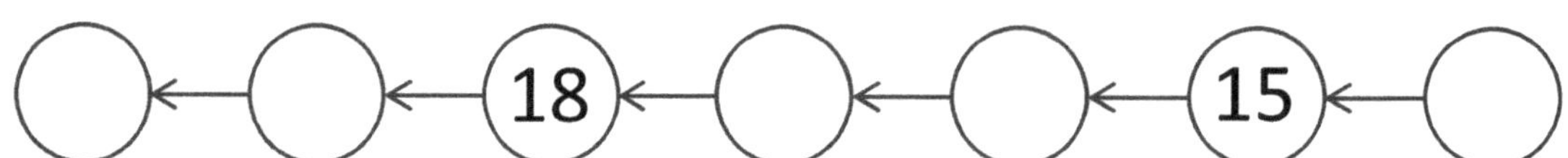

◯ ← ◯ ← ◯ ← 4 ← 3 ← ◯ ← ◯

◯ ← 19 ← 18 ← ◯ ← ◯ ← ◯ ← ◯

COUNTING UP TO 100

Name: _________________________________ **Score:** _______________

Count and write the numbers of blocks in numerals

COUNTING CONES

Name: _________________________________ **Score:** _______________

Count and write the numbers of cones in standard form

COUNTING CONES

Name: ________________________________   **Score:** _______________

Count and write the numbers of cones in standard form

Name: ________________________________ **Score:** ______________

Count and write the numbers of cones in words

_______________ _______________ _______________

_______________ _______________ _______________

_______________ _______________ _______________

Name: ___________________________________ **Score:** _______________

Count the ducks in each set

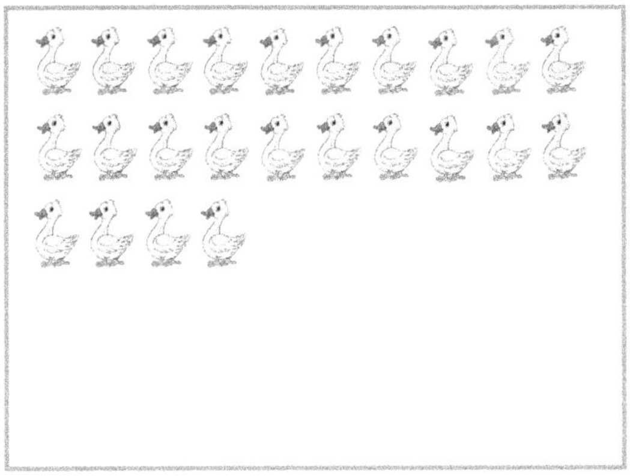

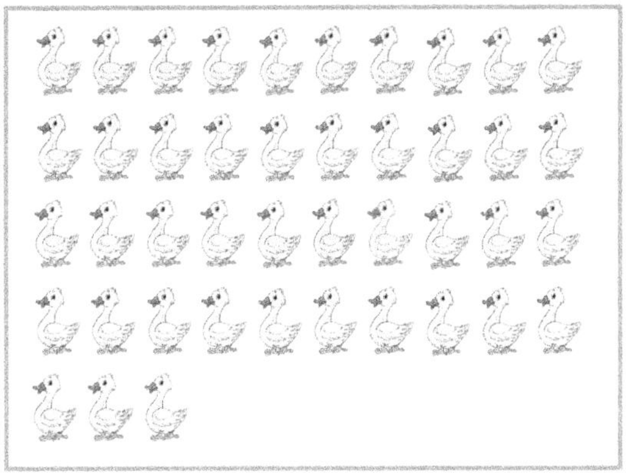

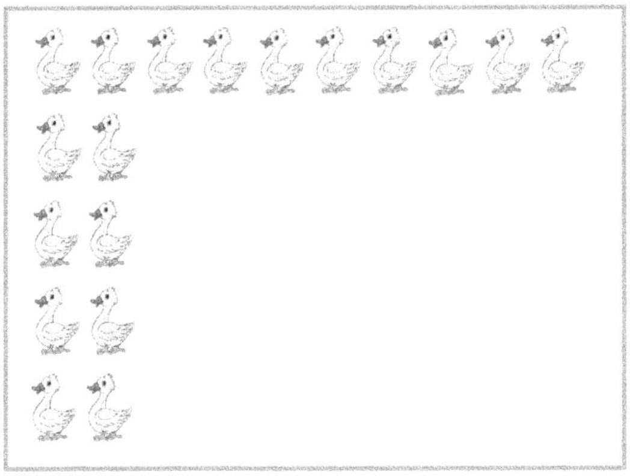

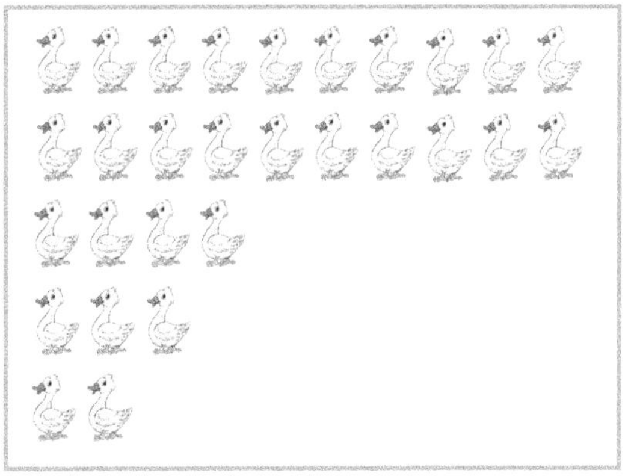

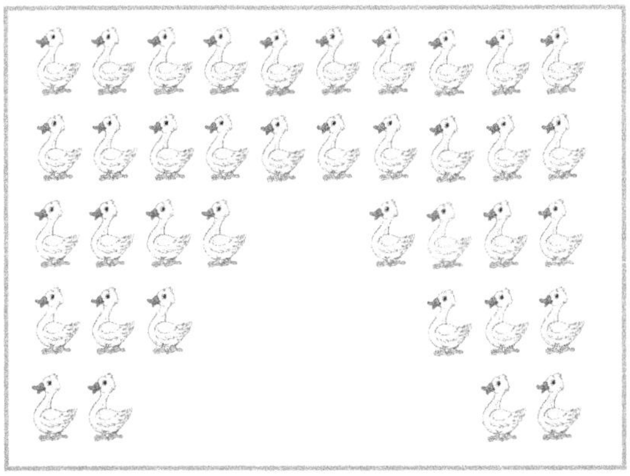

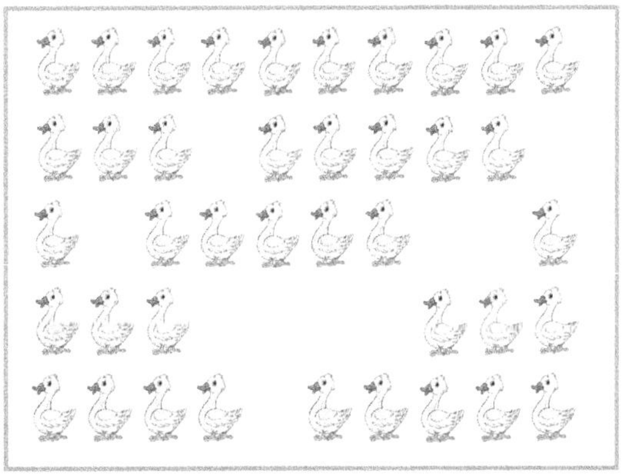

COUNTING COUNTERS

Name: ________________________________ **Score:** ______________

Count the counters in each set

Name: _______________________________ **Score:** _____________

Complete the hundred charts

1			4						
								19	20
		23	24	25					
31									40
			45	46	47				
								59	60
	72	73							
					86				
91	92								
									100

Name: _________________________________ **Score:** _______________

Count forward in each row and complete the empty spaces

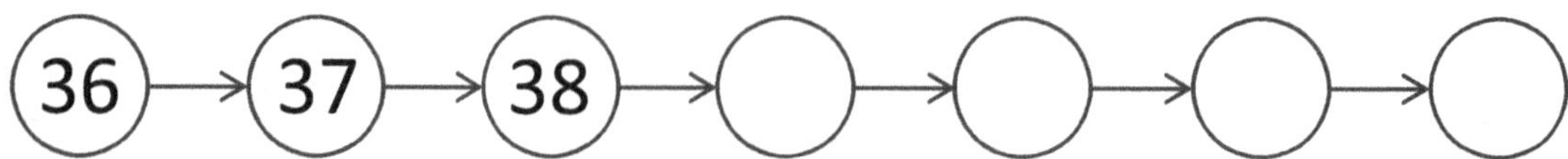

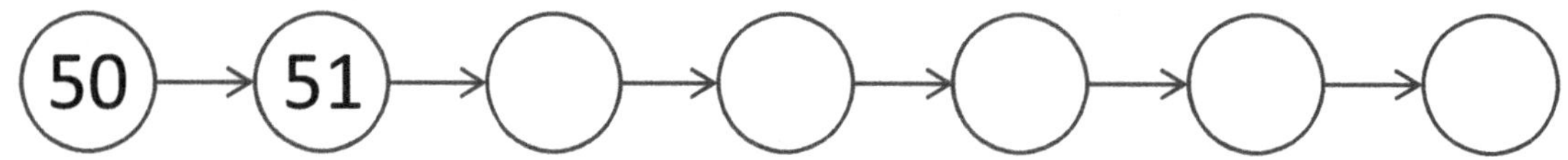

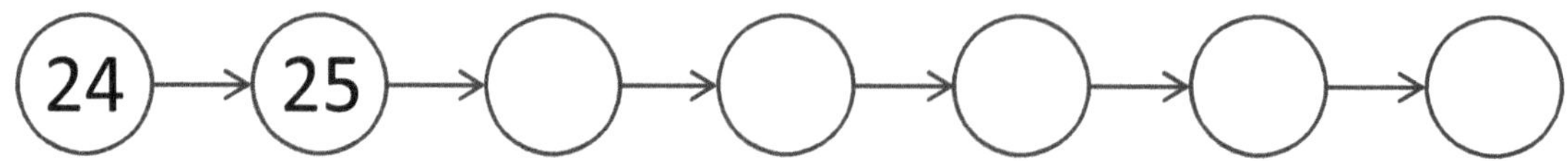

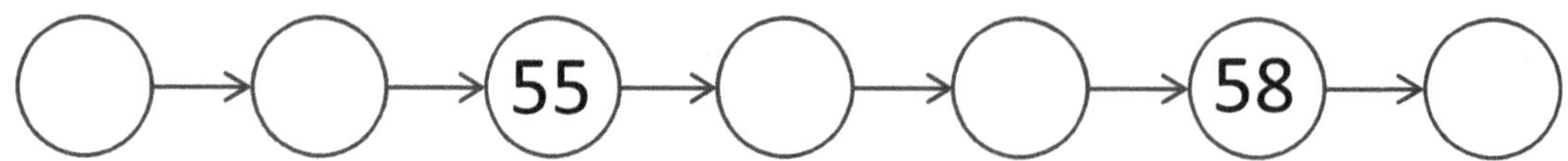

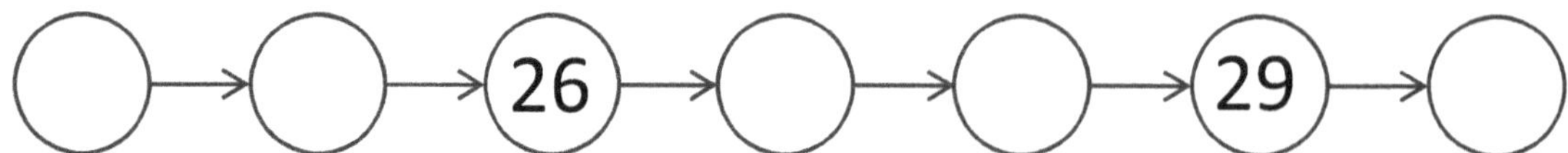

○ → ○ → 26 → ○ → ○ → 29 → ○

COUNTING BACKWARD

Name: _________________________________ **Score:** _______________

Count backward in each row and complete the empty spaces

(7) Count backward from 11 to 5

(11) ← ( ) ← ( ) ← ( ) ← ( ) ← ( ) ← (5)

(6) Count backward from 11 to …

(15) ← ( ) ← ( ) ← ( ) ← ( ) ← ( ) ← ( )

(5) Count backward from 78 to ….

(78) ← ( ) ← ( ) ← ( ) ← ( ) ← ( ) ← ( )

(4) Count backward from … to 39

( ) ← ( ) ← ( ) ← ( ) ← ( ) ← ( ) ← (39)

(3) Count backward from 55 to …

( ) ← ( ) ← (53) ← ( ) ← ( ) ← ( ) ← ( )

(2) Count backward from 92 to ….

( ) ← (91) ← ( ) ← ( ) ← ( ) ← ( ) ← ( )

(1) Count backward from 68 to ….

( ) ← ( ) ← (66) ← ( ) ← ( ) ← ( ) ← ( )

Name: ________________________________ **Score:** ________________

Fill in the missing numbers

Count from 1 to 20									
1	2								
									20

Count from 21 to 40									
21									
	32								40

Count from 41 to 60									
51								59	60

Count from 61 to 80									
					66				
							78		

Count from 81 to 100									
		83							
91									

BEFORE AND AFTER

Name: ___________________________ **Score:** ___________

Fill in the missing number that comes before and after each number

BEFORE AND AFTER

Name: ______________________________ **Score:** ______________

Fill in the missing number that comes before and after each number

BEFORE AND AFTER

Name: _________________________________ **Score:** _______________

Fill in the missing number that comes before and after each number

BEFORE AND AFTER

Name: _______________________________ **Score:** _____________

Fill in the missing number that comes before and after each number

Name: _______________________________ **Score:** _______________

Read carefully and write the answer

I am a number between 0 and 15.
I am the half of 10.
What number am I?

Answer: [ ]

I am a number between 9 and 15.
If you count in 3's you will find me.
What number am I?

Answer: [ ]

I am a number between 20 and 40.
I am half of 60.
What number am I?

Answer: [ ]

I am more than 13 and less than 23.
If you count in 6's you will find me.
What number am I?

Answer: [ ]

I am even number between 20 and 25.
If you count in 3's you will find me.
What number am I?

Answer: [ ]

I am more than 15 and less than 25.
If you count in 5's you will find me.
What number am I?

Answer: [ ]

I am odd number between 10 and 20.
You can divide me by 3.
What number am I?

Answer: [ ]

I am odd number.
I am 3 more than the sum of 2 and 4
What number am I?

Answer: [ ]

You will find me if you subtract 10
from the sum of 20 and 10.
What number am I?

Answer: [ ]

I am more than 30 and less than sum
of 28 and 12. You can divide me by 5.
What number am I?

Answer: [ ]

SPELLING UP TO 20

Name: _______________________________ **Score:** _____________

Count, color and write the number of objects in words

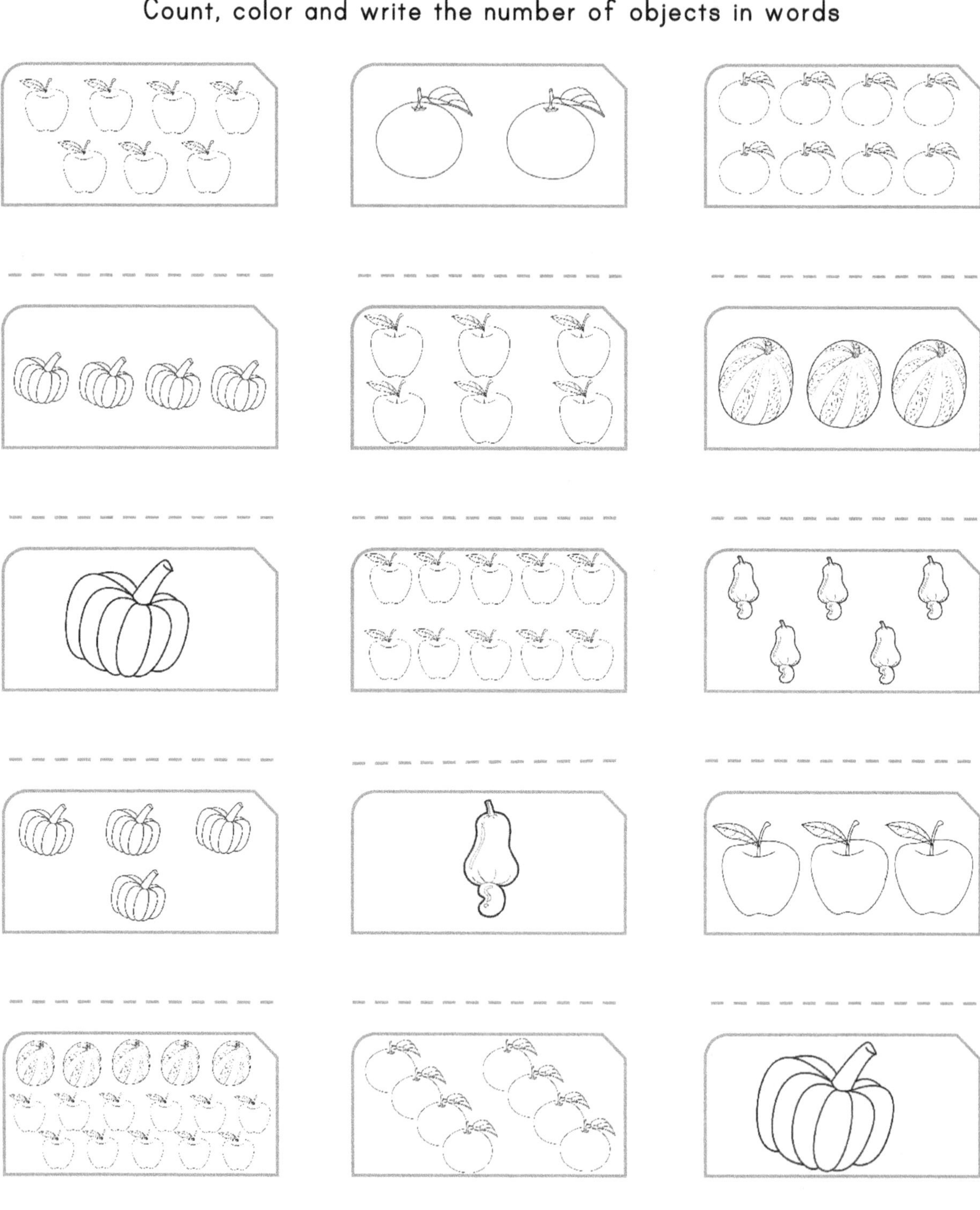

Name: _________________________________ **Score:** _______________

Count, color and write the number of objects in figures

Name: _________________________________ **Score:** _______________

Count, color and write the number of objects in figures

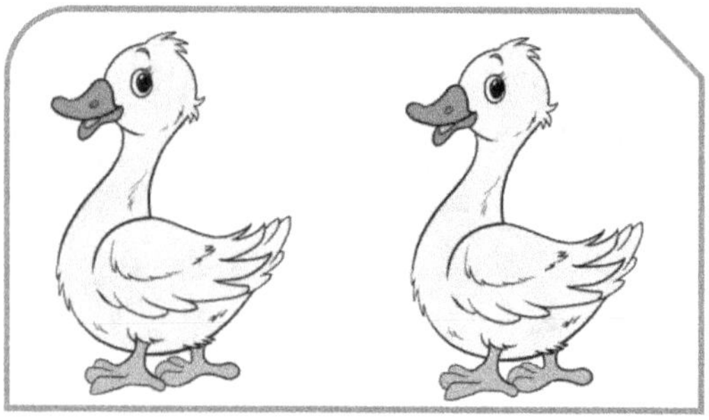

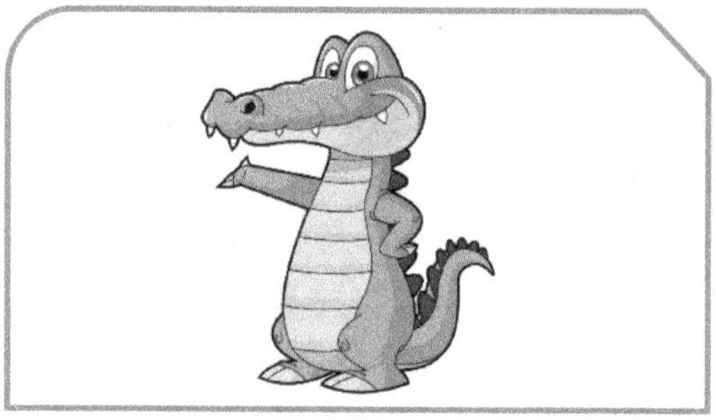

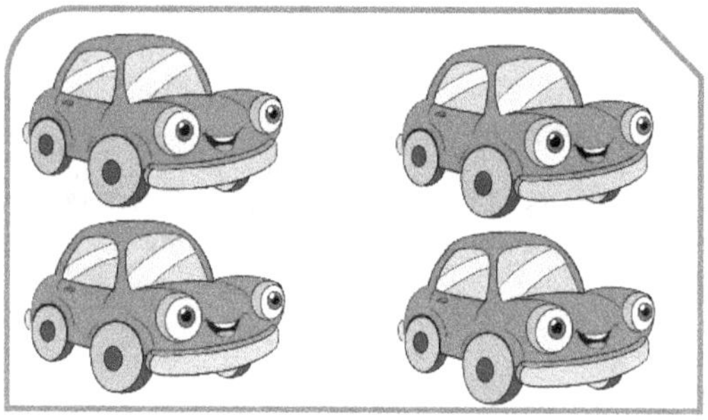

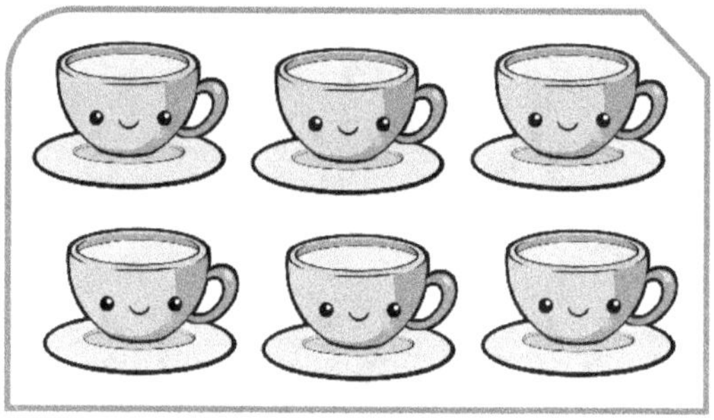

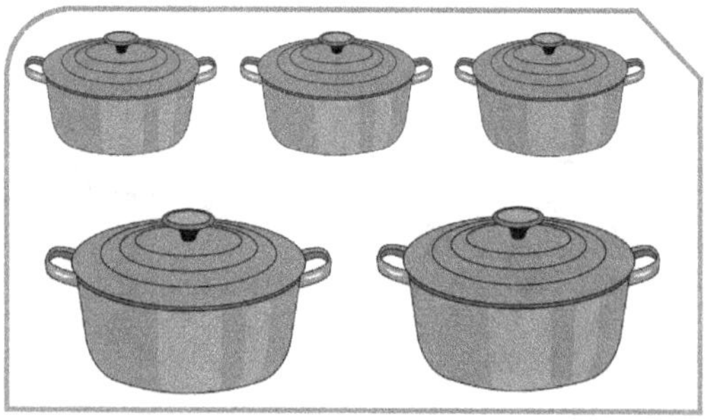

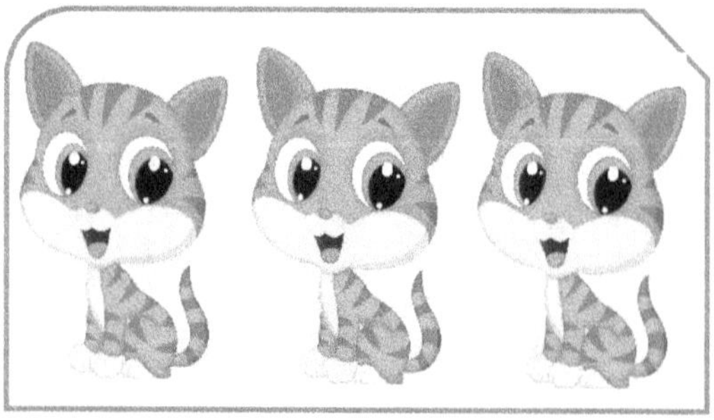

Name: _______________________________ **Score:** _____________

Count, color and write the number of objects in figures

1 2 3 4 5 6 7 8 9 10

1 2 3 4 5 6 7 8 9 10

1 2 3 4 5 6 7 8 9 10

1 2 3 4 5 6 7 8 9 10

1 2 3 4 5 6 7 8 9 10

1 2 3 4 5 6 7 8 9 10

Name: ________________________________ **Score:** _____________

Trace the number words and write the numerals or operator in the rectangle

6	SIX			SEVEN
	MINUS			PLUS
	TWO			FOUR
	NINE			EIGHT
	THREE			FIVE

COUNT AND SPELLING UP TO 10

Name: _________________________________ **Score:** _______________

Count and write the number

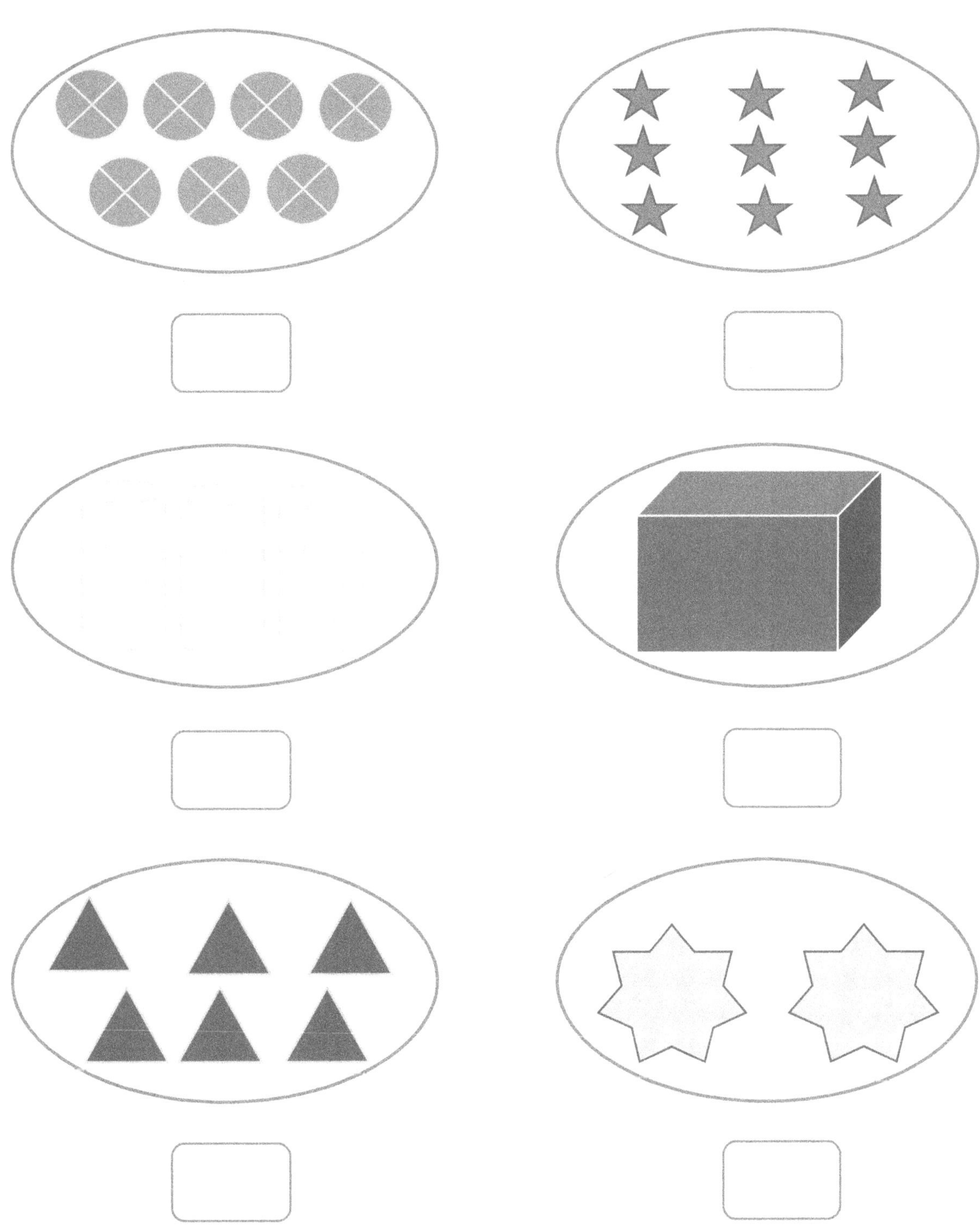

Name: _________________________________ **Score:** _______________

Match the number to the number words

5	●	●	SEVEN
7	●	●	FIVE
4	●	●	SIX
9	●	●	TWO
6	●	●	FOUR
2	●	●	NINE

NUMBER WORDS UP TO 10

Name: _________________________________ **Score:** _______________

Circle the correct spelling

1 | one | five | seven | two | ten | four | six | eight | nine | three

2 | one | five | seven | two | ten | four | six | eight | nine | three

3 | one | five | seven | two | ten | four | six | eight | nine | three

4 | one | five | seven | two | ten | four | six | eight | nine | three

5 | one | five | seven | two | ten | four | six | eight | nine | three

6 | one | five | seven | two | ten | four | six | eight | nine | three

7 | one | five | seven | two | ten | four | six | eight | nine | three

8 | one | five | seven | two | ten | four | six | eight | nine | three

9 | one | five | seven | two | ten | four | six | eight | nine | three

NUMBER WORDS UP TO 10

Name: ______________________ **Score:** __________

Complete the number words

1

O _ E

2

_ W _

3

T _ R _ _

4

F _ _ R

5

_ _ V _

6

S _ _

7

_ _ V E _

8

_ _ G H _

9

_ I _ E

10

_ E _

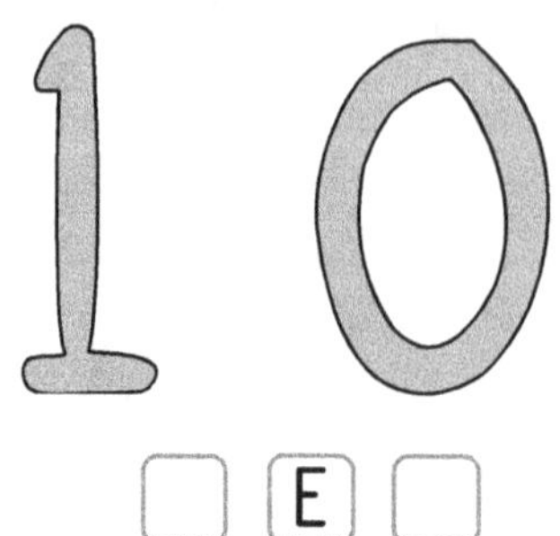

TRACING UP TO 10

Name: _______________________________ **Score:** _____________

Trace the number words and write the numerals or operator in the rectangle

20	TWENTY		ELEVEN
FOURTEEN			SIXNTEEN
SEVEN			NINETEEN
SEVENTEEN			THIRTEEN
SIX			NINE

Name: ________________________________ **Score:** ______________

Write the following numbers in words

12	__________	11	__________
20	__________	3	__________
18	__________	10	__________
17	__________	8	__________
13	__________	7	__________
15	__________	16	__________
14	__________	1	__________
19	__________	5	__________

Name: _________________________________ **Score:** _______________

Write the following numbers in words

Name: ________________________________ **Score:** ______________

Count the blocks and write the numbers and number words

cv

NUMBER WORDS UP TO 20

Name: _________________________________ **Score:** _______________

Use the table and write the numbers in words

thirteen	sixteen	fourteen	twenty	thirteen	seventeen
eleven	fifteen	nineteen	twelve	thirteen	eighteen
six	ten	four	five		

17 _______________

12 _______________

14 _______________

16 _______________

15 _______________

6 _______________

10 _______________

13 _______________

18 _______________

20 _______________

19 _______________

11 _______________

5 _______________

4 _______________

Name: ________________________________ **Score:** ______________

Circle the right number

seventeen	**fifteen**	**fourteen**
17 19 18	13 12 15	4 14 13
twelve	**eleven**	**thirteen**
11 12 13	11 12 13	11 12 13
sixteen	**twenty**	**ten**
15 14 16	17 18 20	9 10 11

Match the number to the number words

4	ONE
1	THREE
7	FOUR
3	EIGHT
8	SEVEN
6	SIX

Match the number to the number words

15 ●	● TWELVE
12 ●	● FOURTEEN
18 ●	● FIFTEEN
14 ●	● NINETEEN
19 ●	● TWENTY
20 ●	● EIGHTEEN

Name: _______________________________ **Score:** _____________

Add the numbers and complete the spelling

15 + 2 = ☐

N I
12 + 7 = ☐

9 + 2 = ☐

E I   H T
10 + 8 = ☐

10 + 3 = ☐

S I   N
8 + 8 = ☐

10 + 10 = ☐

O U   T   N
7 + 7 = ☐

MISSING NUMBERS UP TO 50

Name: ______________________________ **Score:** _____________

Complete the missing numbers in words

TWENTY-TWO	TWENTY-THREE	TWENTY-FOUR	TWENTY-FIVE
SIXTEEN	SEVENTEEN		
THIRTY-TWO	THIRTY-THREE		
EIGHTEEN	NINETEEN		
FORTY-SIX		FORTY-EIGHT	
	TWENTY-SEVEN		TWENTY-NINE

Name: _______________________________ **Score:** _______________

Write the following numbers in words

16 _______________________   26 _______________________

37 _______________________   13 _______________________

42 _______________________   29 _______________________

11 _______________________   38 _______________________

50 _______________________   23 _______________________

15 _______________________   31 _______________________

19 _______________________   14 _______________________

46 _______________________   34 _______________________

25 _______________________   45 _______________________

Name: _______________________________ **Score:** _______________

Write the following numbers in words

88 ________________	99 ________________
32 ________________	47 ________________
55 ________________	30 ________________
85 ________________	51 ________________
77 ________________	94 ________________
36 ________________	69 ________________
44 ________________	29 ________________
100 ________________	92 ________________
73 ________________	60 ________________

Name: ___________________________ **Score:** _____________

Write the following numbers in words

43	___________________	77	___________________
27	___________________	85	___________________
74	___________________	35	___________________
81	___________________	51	___________________
18	___________________	21	___________________
96	___________________	54	___________________
61	___________________	32	___________________
87	___________________	95	___________________
83	___________________	65	___________________

Name: ________________________________ **Score:** ______________

Circle the right number

Seventy-two	hundred	Thirty-nine
7 72 71	98 99 100	38 40 39

Thirty-six	Twenty-nine	Forty-eight
36 38 37	29 31 30	48 49 47

Sixty-four	Fifty-five	Ninety-two
62 64 63	54 55 56	91 90 92

Name: _________________________________ **Score:** _______________

Circle the number in the grid containing the following numbers

Thirty-eight	Thirty-seven	Sixty-six
Fifty-three	Forty-three	Twenty-seven
Hundred	Fifty-nine	Sixty-seven
Fifty-six	Sixty-two	Twenty-nine
Forty-eight	Forty	Twenty-eight
Thirty-two	Sixty-three	Ninety
Seventy-seven	Fifty	Twenty-six

38	39	66	42	43	44	100	40
15	16	17	18	91	92	80	81
67	68	56	57	62	64	29	30
48	49	40	41	52	54	32	33
63	65	66	76	77	78	50	55
24	25	26	31	34	28	35	36
37	51	53	61	88	90	89	87
71	72	27	73	74	75	59	60

NUMBER WORDS UP TO 100

Name: ________________________________ **Score:** ______________

Write the numbers in the box space

Thirty-eight	→ ☐	Forty-nine	→ ☐
Seventy-two	→ ☐	Eighty-three	→ ☐
Seventy-four	→ ☐	Ninety-five	→ ☐
Ninety-nine	→ ☐	Ninety	→ ☐
Twenty-seven	→ ☐	Thirty-four	→ ☐
Forty-six	→ ☐	Fifty-five	→ ☐
Fifty-seven	→ ☐	Sixty-six	→ ☐
Eighty-three	→ ☐	Twenty-five	→ ☐
Thirty	→ ☐	Ninety-seven	→ ☐
Ninety-two	→ ☐	Thirty-nine	→ ☐
Forty-five	→ ☐	Seventy-six	→ ☐
Sixty-nine	→ ☐	Fifty-two	→ ☐
Eighty-nine	→ ☐	Seventy-eight	→ ☐
Sixty-seven	→ ☐	Ninety-six	→ ☐
Fifty-three	→ ☐	Fifty-nine	→ ☐

Match the number to the number words

82	FORTY-THREE
43	SIXTY-SIX
62	FIFTY-FIVE
66	THIRTY-FOUR
34	EIGHTY-TWO
55	SIXTY-TWO

NUMBER WORDS UP TO 100

Match the number to the number words

57	TWENTY-EIGHT
28	FORTY-SEVEN
62	FIFTY-SEVEN
98	SIXTY-TWO
47	NINETY-EIGHT
55	FIFTY-FIVE

Name: _________________________________ **Score:** _____________

Use the table bank and write the numbers in words

Ten	Twenty	Thirty	Forty	Fifty	Sixty
Seventy	Eighty	Ninety	Hundred	Twenty-five	
Thirty-five		Forty-five		Fifty-five	

10 _______________________

20 _______________________

30 _______________________

40 _______________________

50 _______________________

60 _______________________

70 _______________________

80 _______________________

90 _______________________

100 _______________________

25 _______________________

35 _______________________

45 _______________________

55 _______________________

Name: ________________________________ **Score:** ______________

Circle the right spelling of each number

Ten Twenty Thirty **10**	Ten Twenty Thirty **20**	Ten Twenty Thirty **30**
Thirty Forty Fifty **40**	Fifty Sixty Seventy **50**	Fifty Sixty Seventy **60**
Seventy Eighty Ninety **70**	Sixty Seventy Eighty **80**	Seventy Eighty Ninety **90**

NUMBER WORDS UP TO 100

Name: ______________________________ **Score:** _____________

Complete the number spelling

10

_ E _

20

_ _ E N _ _

30

T _ _ R _ _

40

F _ _ T Y

50

_ I F _ _

60

S _ X _ _

70

S _ V _ _ _ Y

80

E _ _ H _ _

90

N _ N _ _ _

100

_ U N _ _ _ _

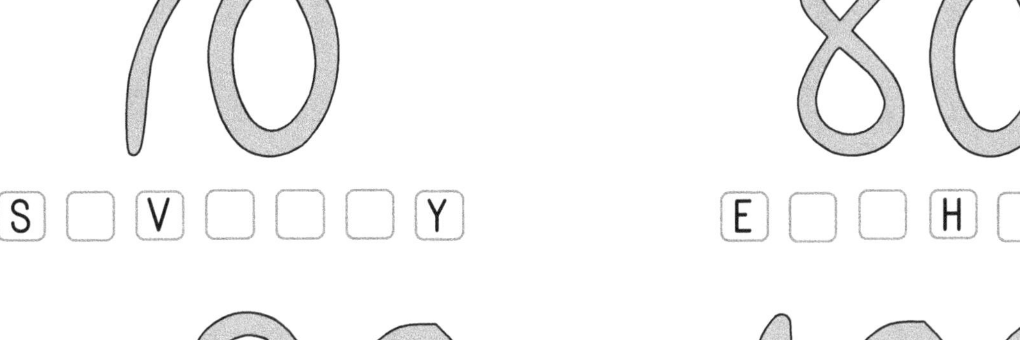

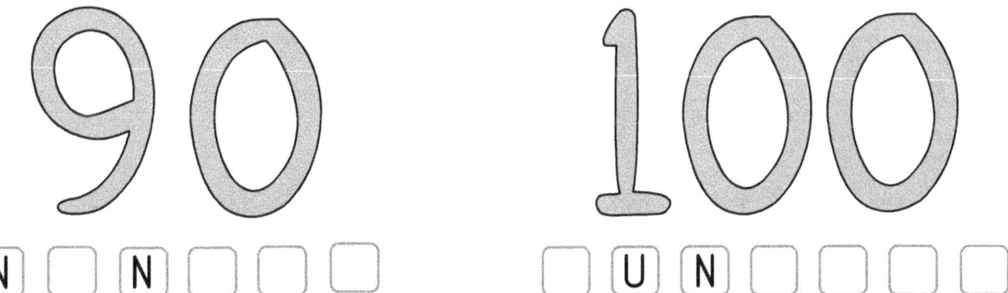

Name: _________________________________ **Score:** _______________

Add the numbers and spell the answer in words

11 + 6	_________________________
17 - 8	_________________________
9 + 5	_________________________
19 - 2	_________________________
18 - 3	_________________________
11 + 1	_________________________
15 - 6	_________________________
20 - 8	_________________________
10 + 2	_________________________
12 + 6	_________________________

Name: _______________________________ **Score:** _______________

Add the numbers and spell the answer in words

| 10 + 8 | _______________________________ |

| 16 - 7 | _______________________________ |

| 21 + 8 | _______________________________ |

| 9 - 1 | _______________________________ |

| 19 - 5 | _______________________________ |

| 18 + 1 | _______________________________ |

| 15 - 8 | _______________________________ |

| 25 - 7 | _______________________________ |

| 11 + 6 | _______________________________ |

| 17 - 8 | _______________________________ |

COUNTING EVEN AND ODD SHAPES

Name: ________________________________ **Score:** ______________

Color and count the shapes in the box and trace the correct answer even or odd

Odd Even

Odd Even

Odd Even

Odd Even

Odd Even

Odd Even

COUNTING EVEN AND ODD PICTURES

Name: _________________________________ **Score:** _______________

Count the shapes and write if it's even or odd

How many cars? _____10_____

Odd or Even _Even_

How many cats? _________

Odd or Even _________

How many Trees? _________

Odd or Even _________

How many Ducks? _________

Odd or Even _________

How many Mangoes? ___________

Odd or Even ___________

How many Pots? ___________

Odd or Even ___________

Name: ________________________________ **Score:** _______________

Count the shapes and write if it's even or odd

How many Cups? ___6___

Odd or Even _Even_

How many Caps? ________

Odd or Even ________

How many Umbrellas? __________

Odd or Even __________

How many Fishes? ________

Odd or Even ________

How many Dogs? __________

Odd or Even ________

How many Kettles? __________

Odd or Even __________

Name: _________________________________ **Score:** _______________

Shade the even numbers in the box below

38	13	50	99	78	90	82	24	17	30	30	84
37	52	67	100	94	27	19	41	66	45	34	18

Shade the odd numbers in the box below

57	49	40	42	45	81	94	56	17	96	87	75
38	41	52	89	59	72	64	29	35	67	16	91

Shade the odd numbers in the box below

1	2	3	4	5	6	7	8	9	10	81	12

Shade the even numbers in the box below

13	14	15	16	17	18	19	20	21	22	23	24

Shade the odd numbers in the box below

25	26	27	28	29	30	31	32	33	34	35	36

Name: ____ **Score:** __________________

Shade or Circle the even numbers in the box below

23	34	22	19	75	30	38	82	40	45	90
18	17	34	56	89	27	36	81	54	98	14
39	24	46	30	92	26	67	78	99	11	34
52	56	18	21	59	76	44	25	90	37	72
100	50	93	43	86	77	28	82	21	69	98

Shade or Circle the odd numbers in the box below

25	33	24	20	73	28	40	84	35	46	88
14	19	74	66	90	26	31	82	57	96	20
38	25	55	29	100	78	64	77	68	11	12
58	96	38	61	52	36	94	45	30	17	82
50	43	13	48	19	15	72	28	98	21	71

Name: _________________________________ **Score:** _______________

Color all the even numbers green and odd numbers yellow in the box below

1	2	3	4	5	6	7	8	9	10
11	12	13	14	15	16	17	18	19	20
21	22	23	24	25	26	27	28	29	30
31	32	33	34	35	36	37	38	39	40
41	42	43	44	45	46	47	48	49	50
51	52	53	54	55	56	57	58	59	60
61	62	63	64	65	66	67	68	69	70
71	72	73	74	75	76	77	78	79	80
81	82	83	84	85	86	87	88	89	90
91	92	93	94	95	96	97	98	99	100

Name: _________________________________ **Score:** _______________

Color or shade all the boxes with even numbers

34	39

57	58

68	77

39	32

76	77

29	86

45	46

94	95

29	86

52	51

89	88

99	90

Color or shade all the boxes with odd numbers

93	94

27	22

67	66

18	21

51	52

67	66

58	57

89	90

55	56

33	34

28	25

29	30

COUNTING EVEN AND ODD NUMBERS

Name: _________________________________   Score: _______________

Circle odd or even for each number

Odd Even	34	Odd Even	43	Odd Even	56
Odd Even	59	Odd Even	48	Odd Even	71
Odd Even	62	Odd Even	99	Odd Even	88
Odd Even	75	Odd Even	66	Odd Even	83
Odd Even	68	Odd Even	17	Odd Even	92
Odd Even	24	Odd Even	45	Odd Even	77
Odd Even	55	Odd Even	22	Odd Even	33
Odd Even	92	Odd Even	44	Odd Even	91
Odd Even	21	Odd Even	12	Odd Even	100

Name: ________________________________ **Score:** _______________

Shade or Circle the even numbers in the box below

25	36	24	21	77	32	40	84	42	47	92
20	19	36	58	91	29	38	83	56	100	16
41	26	48	32	94	28	69	80	97	13	36
54	58	18	23	61	78	46	27	92	39	74
39	52	95	45	88	79	30	84	23	71	98

Shade or Circle the odd numbers in the box below

27	35	26	22	75	30	42	86	37	48	90
16	21	76	68	92	28	33	84	59	98	22
40	27	57	31	100	80	66	79	70	11	14
60	96	38	63	54	39	94	45	32	19	84
52	46	13	47	19	15	72	44	99	47	20

Name: _______________________________ **Score:** _______________

Place the numbers below in the odd or even box

56	47	74	85	62	51
45	78	95	86	19	34
68	77	82	59	66	13
20	37	90	71	26	11
18	39	88	73	24	16

Name: _______________________________ **Score:** _______________

Tell whether the numbers are odd or even. Then find the answer. Is the sum odd or even?

4 + 1 = <u>Odd + Even</u> = <u>5</u>, <u>5</u> is an <u>Odd</u> number.

3 + 7 = _____________ = ___, ___ is an _________ number.

2 + 6 = _____________ = ___, ___ is an _________ number.

10 + 5 = _____________ = ___, ___ is an _________ number.

14 + 4 = _____________ = ___, ___ is an _________ number.

9 + 20 = _____________ = ___, ___ is an _________ number.

12 + 11 = _____________ = ___, ___ is an _________ number.

13 + 7 = _____________ = ___, ___ is an _________ number.

Name: _________________________________ **Score:** _____________

Tell whether the numbers are odd or even. Then find the answer. Is the sum odd or even?

4 + 1 = <u>Odd + Even</u> = <u>5</u>, <u>5</u> is an <u>Odd</u> number.

8 + 9 = _______________ = ___, ___ is an _________ number.

6 + 6 = _______________ = ___, ___ is an _________ number.

15 + 11 = _______________ = ___, ___ is an _________ number.

20 + 16 = _______________ = ___, ___ is an _________ number.

13 + 18 = _______________ = ___, ___ is an _________ number.

15 + 26 = _______________ = ___, ___ is an _________ number.

23 + 19 = _______________ = ___, ___ is an _________ number.

EVEN AND ODD? PRACTICE ADDITION

Name: _________________________________ **Score:** _______________

Tell whether the numbers are odd or even. Then find the answer. Is the sum odd or even?

4 + 1   = __Odd + Even__   = _5_, _5_ is an __Odd__ number.

26 + 12   = ______________   = ___, ___ is an ________ number.

39 + 16   = ______________   = ___, ___ is an ________ number.

13 + 37   = ______________   = ___, ___ is an ________ number.

55 + 20   = ______________   = ___, ___ is an ________ number.

6 + 7   = ______________   = ___, ___ is an ________ number.

9 + 9   = ______________   = ___, ___ is an ________ number.

12 + 6   = ______________   = ___, ___ is an ________ number.

9 + 14   = ______________   = ___, ___ is an ________ number.

18 + 7   = ______________   = ___, ___ is an ________ number.

16 + 12   = ______________   = ___, ___ is an ________ number.

Name: ______________________________ **Score:** ______________

Tell whether the numbers are odd or even. Then find the answer. Is the sum odd or even?

4 + 1   = _Odd + Even_   = _5_, _5_ is an _Odd_ number.

10 + 14   = ______________   = ___, ___ is an ________ number.

17 + 18   = ______________   = ___, ___ is an ________ number.

11 + 37   = ______________   = ___, ___ is an ________ number.

25 + 25   = ______________   = ___, ___ is an ________ number.

55 + 6   = ______________   = ___, ___ is an ________ number.

13 + 8   = ______________   = ___, ___ is an ________ number.

19 + 9   = ______________   = ___, ___ is an ________ number.

Name: _________________________________ **Score:** _______________

Tell whether the numbers are odd or even. Then find the answer. Is the difference odd or even?

4 - 1 = <u>Odd + Even</u> = <u>3</u>, <u>3</u> is an <u>Odd</u> number.

9 - 3 = ______________ = ___, ___ is an _________ number.

10 - 1 = ______________ = ___, ___ is an _________ number.

12 - 8 = ______________ = ___, ___ is an _________ number.

13 - 2 = ______________ = ___, ___ is an _________ number.

32 - 9 = ______________ = ___, ___ is an _________ number.

24 - 6 = ______________ = ___, ___ is an _________ number.

20 - 7 = ______________ = ___, ___ is an _________ number.

Name: ______________________________ **Score:** ______________

Tell whether the numbers are odd or even. Then find the answer. Is the difference odd or even?

4 - 1 = <u>Odd + Even</u> = <u>3</u>, <u>3</u> is an <u>Odd</u> number.

44 - 5 = ______________ = ___, ___ is an ________ number.

33 - 9 = ______________ = ___, ___ is an ________ number.

10 - 7 = ______________ = ___, ___ is an ________ number.

11 - 1 = ______________ = ___, ___ is an ________ number.

30 - 8 = ______________ = ___, ___ is an ________ number.

22 - 5 = ______________ = ___, ___ is an ________ number.

18 - 6 = ______________ = ___, ___ is an ________ number.

Name: _______________________________ **Score:** _______________

Tell whether the numbers are odd or even. Then find the answer. Is the difference odd or even?

4 - 1   = _Odd + Even_   = _3_ , _3_ is an _Odd_ number.

7 - 3   = _______________   = ___ , ___ is an _________ number.

12 - 1   = _______________   = ___ , ___ is an _________ number.

13 - 6   = _______________   = ___ , ___ is an _________ number.

12 - 6   = _______________   = ___ , ___ is an _________ number.

21 - 8   = _______________   = ___ , ___ is an _________ number.

25 - 9   = _______________   = ___ , ___ is an _________ number.

24 - 4   = _______________   = ___ , ___ is an _________ number.

23 - 5   = _______________   = ___ , ___ is an _________ number.

44 - 5   = _______________   = ___ , ___ is an _________ number.

22 - 9   = _______________   = ___ , ___ is an _________ number.

40 - 9   = _______________   = ___ , ___ is an _________ number.

Name: ___________________________________ **Score:** _______________

Read and learn the ordinal numbers up to 20

ORDINAL NUMBERS

1st first	2nd Second	3rd Third	4th Fourth	5th Fifth
6th Sixth	7th Seventh	8th Eighth	9th Ninth	10th Tenth
11th Eleventh	12th Twelfth	13th Thirteenth	14th Fourteenth	15th Fifteenth
16th Sixteenth	17th Seventeenth	18th Eighteenth	19th Nineteenth	20th Twentieth

ORDINAL NUMBERS

Name: _________________________________ **Score:** _____________

(a) Color the first apple in the row

(b) Color the third orange in the row

(c) Color the second mango in the row

(d) Color the fifth pawpaw in the row

(e) Color the fourth watermelon in the row

(f) Color the fourth cashew in the row

ORDINAL NUMBERS

Name: ______________________________ **Score:** ____________

(a) Color the last three apples blue and color the first red. Put a X on the second, third and fourth apples.

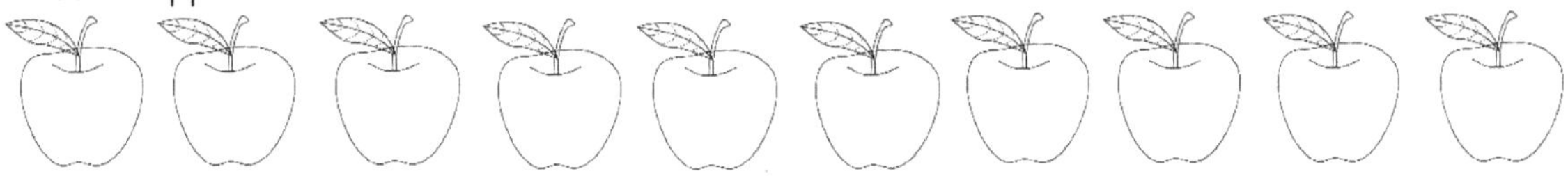

(b) Put an X on the second, fourth and eight. Color the first, third and tenth orange yellow

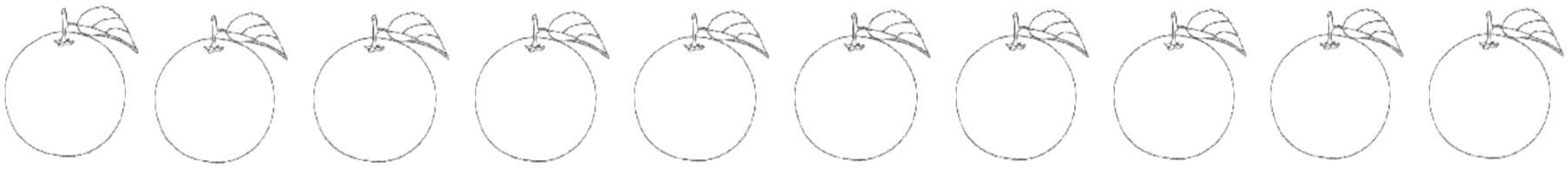

(c) Put an X on the fourth, fifth and sixth mango. Color the first, second and tenth mango green

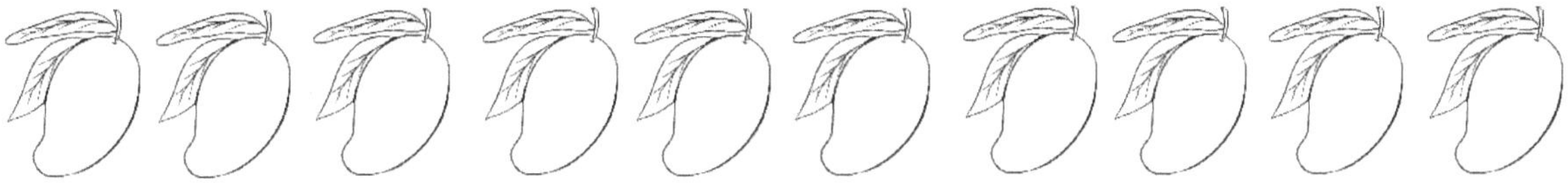

(d) Put an Y on the second and last pawpaw. Color the first, fourth and sixth pawpaw yellow

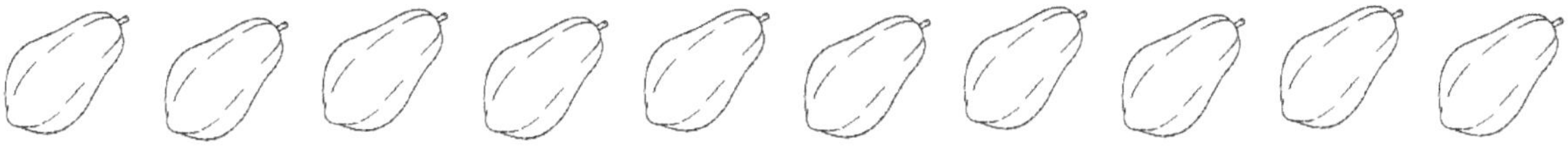

(e) Put an X on the fourth and fifth water melon. Color the fist and eight water melon green

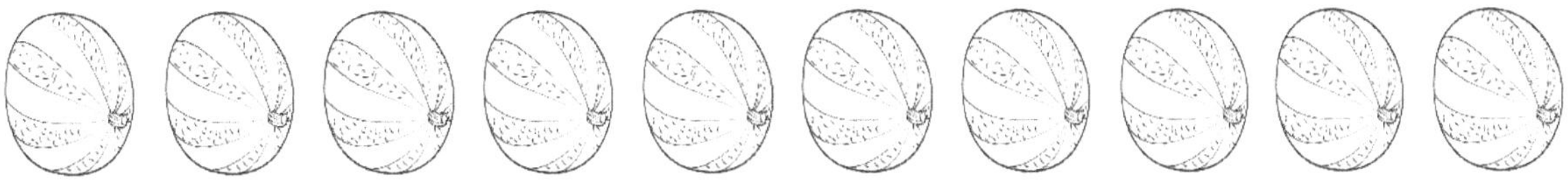

(f) Put an Y on the nineth and fifth water cashew. Color the first and third cashew green

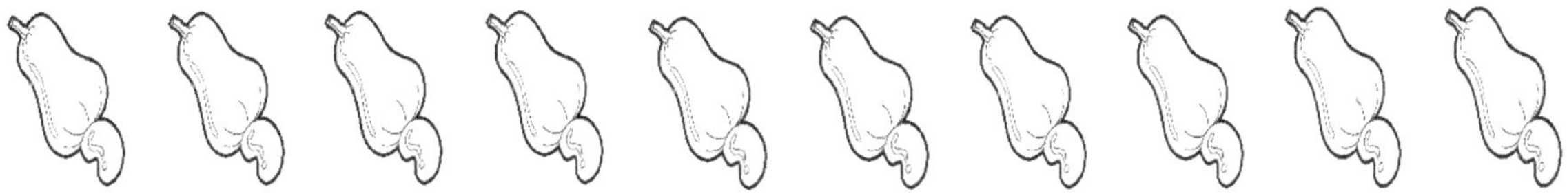

ORDINAL NUMBERS

Name: ______________________________ **Score:** _____________

(a) Cross out the second and third duck. Circle the first and last duck.

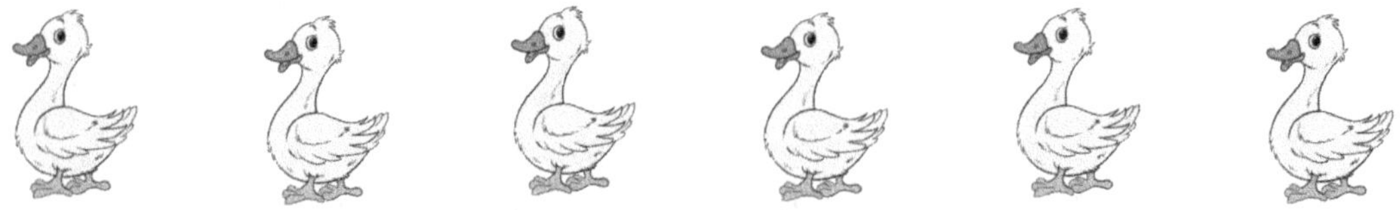

(b) Cross out the first and second dog. Circle the third and fifth dog

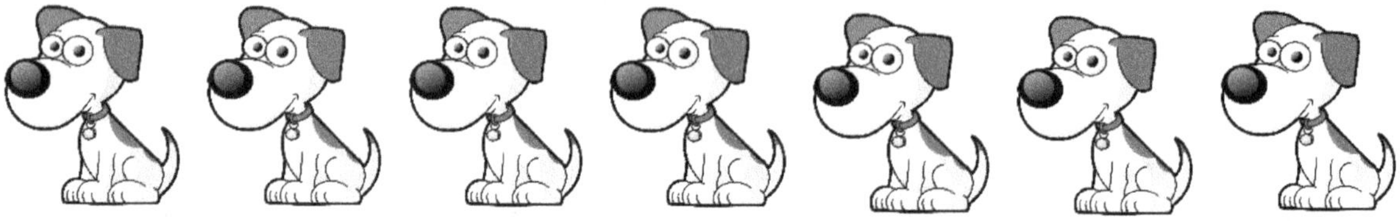

(c) Cross out the second, third and fourth kettle. Circle the first kettle.

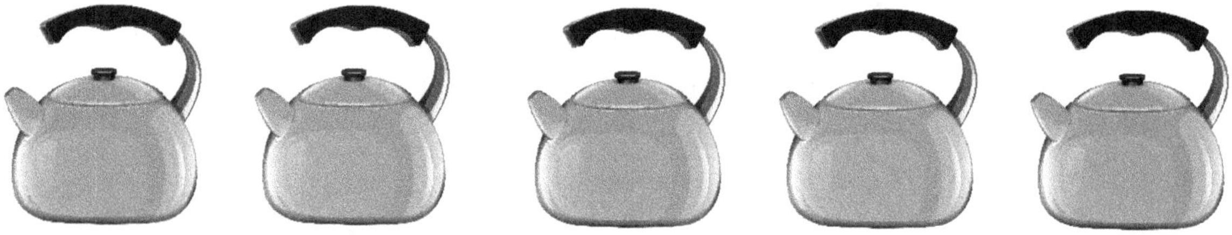

(d) Cross out the fourth, fifth and seventh cap. Circle the second cap

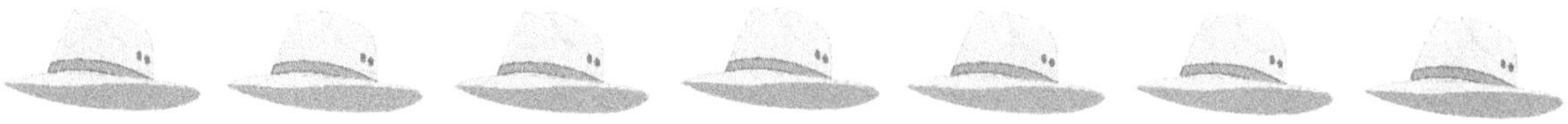

(e) Cross out the third iron. Circle the second, and the last iron

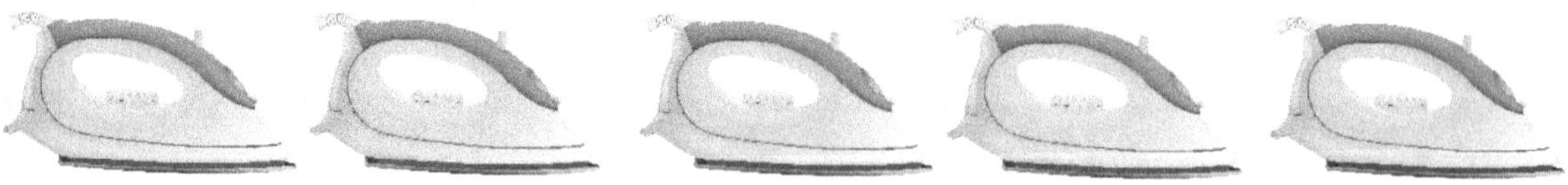

(f) Cross out the first and last umbrella. Circle the third, and the last umbrella

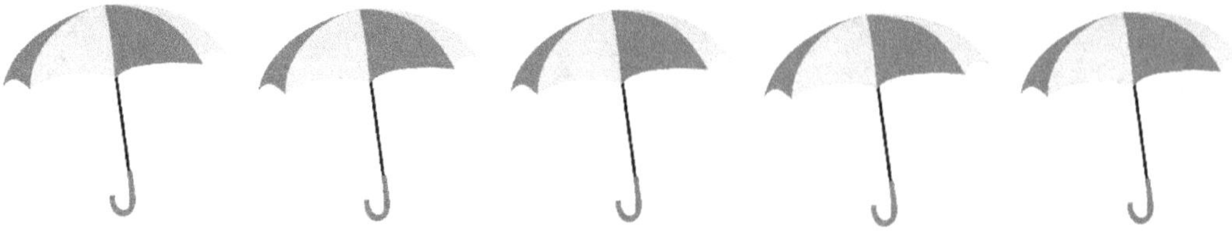

ORDINAL NUMBERS

Name: _________________________________ **Score:** ______________

(a) Color the first apple from the right in the row

(b) Color the first orange from the left in the row

(c) Color the third mango from the right in the row

(d) Color the third pawpaw from the left in the row

(e) Color the fifth watermelon from the right in the row

(f) Color the seventh cashew from the right in the row

Name: _________________________________ **Score:** ______________

Writhe following ordinal numbers in words

1st	First	11th	
2nd		12th	
3rd		13th	
4th		14th	
5th		15th	
6th		16th	
7th		17th	
8th		18th	
9th		19th	
10th		20th	

Name: _________________________________ **Score:** _______________

Draw a line between the ordinal number to its ordinal words

1st	Fourth
2nd	Eighth
3rd	Second
4th	Tenth
5th	First
6th	Third
7th	Ninth
8th	Fifth
9th	Seventh
10th	Sixth

Name: _________________________________ **Score:** _______________

Complete the sentences using an ordinal word. E.g. First, Second etc.

A is the ______________ letter of the Alphabet

I is the ______________ letter of the Alphabet

D is the ______________ letter of the Alphabet

F is the ______________ letter of the Alphabet

J is the ______________ letter of the Alphabet

H is the ______________ letter of the Alphabet

C is the ______________ letter of the Alphabet

G is the ______________ letter of the Alphabet

B is the ______________ letter of the Alphabet

E is the ______________ letter of the Alphabet

Name: _________________________________ **Score:** _______________

Draw a line between the ordinal number to its ordinal words

11th	Fourteenth
12th	Eighteenth
13th	Twelfth
14th	Twentieth
15th	Eleventh
16th	Thirteenth
17th	Nineteenth
18th	Fifteenth
19th	Seventeenth
20th	Sixteenth

Name: _________________________________ **Score:** _______________

Answer the question.

What is the 1st letter from the right in the word CAT? _______

What is the 3rd letter from the left in the word CAT? _______

What is the 4th letter from the left in the word ORANGE? _______

What is the 7th letter from the right in the word UMBRELLA? _______

What is the 5th letter from the left in the word ORANGE? _______

What is the 2nd letter from the right in the word POT? _______

What is the 8th letter from the right in the word MOTORBIKE? _______

What is the 10th letter from the left in the word WATERMELON? _______

What is the 9th letter from the right in the word PINEAPPLE? _______

What is the 6th letter from the right in the word MANGO? _______

ALPHABET ORDINAL NUMBERS

Name: ________________________________ **Score:** ______________

Complete the sentences using an ordinal word. E.g. First, Second etc.

K is the ______________ letter of the Alphabet

S is the ______________ letter of the Alphabet

N is the ______________ letter of the Alphabet

P is the ______________ letter of the Alphabet

T is the ______________ letter of the Alphabet

R is the ______________ letter of the Alphabet

M is the ______________ letter of the Alphabet

Q is the ______________ letter of the Alphabet

L is the ______________ letter of the Alphabet

O is the ______________ letter of the Alphabet

<u>NOTES</u>